# THE
# LADY
## AND
# GIRL
## WITH A
# *Red Kite*

A. Guevara

ISBN 978-1-64670-721-8 (Paperback)
ISBN 978-1-64670-722-5 (Hardcover)
ISBN 978-1-64670-723-2 (Digital)

Grace To You https://www.gty.org/—Online Resources, Sermons
The ESV Study Bible, by Pastor John MacArthur
Fundamentals of the Faith, by Pastor John MacArthur
Thru the Bible Program https://www.ttb.org/ Dr. J. Vernon McGee and free Bible Study outlines and resources.

Covenant Books, Inc.
11661 Hwy 707
Murrells Inlet, SC 29576
www.covenantbooks.com

*For daddy, I am sharing your gift.*
*For Your love is too beautiful to keep.*

# CHAPTER 1

## *Train of Thoughts*

*P*erhaps the world would will permit me to tell,
the story of a little country girl.
Her father sent her to the big city to see.
What was in her heart and who she could be.

Her little heart was thrilled, her big mind accentuated,
what bright promises and eerie risks in the city awaited.
She grabbed for her pad, wrote a letter to her Dad,
as the train churned on, thoughts of home made her sad.

FAITH

what do you
often think
about?

New York Train

3

IF YOU SEE SOMETHING, SAY SOMETHING.
Luke 2:30-32
Land of Opportunity
Bronx
What is your American Dream?
SUBWAY
Life
Manhattan
Liberty &
Pursuit of Happiness
Queens
Brooklyn
Staten Island
Long Island
Easy To Fold!
New York City
streets

Dad,

I am more scared as the train draws near,
But your love and rich trust fund will keep my paths clear.
When I make it to the city, the first thing I will do,
I will fly my Red Kite to tell, "I miss you."
From the mountains that you dwell,
the highest peak my Red Kite—soar to tell,
your love, O Dad, that I know so well.

Sincerely,
Your Daughter

Him being a meticulous Dad,
made her bring his golden pass in her hand.
All food to her liking, sightseeing, and lodging is free.
He just said, "Every time you use it, do think of me."

From the train she stepped down, heart and feet both light,
surveying details of the city's beauty and might.
She caught her breath, for the language was new,
(She whispered)
*Dad, give me wisdom to carry out what I must do.*

## CHAPTER 2

### *The City of Times Fair*

So came tallest buildings—oldest and new.
She smiled at peoples of different races and views.
But there's only one color for the cars on the street?
She called, "Taxi! Taxi!" her heart skipped a beat.

TRUTH

Do you have a roadmap to success?

Taxi

Driver: Oh, Little Girl, where is your first stop?

Li'l Girl: Oh, Mister, I wonder, there are too many shops.

Driver: Hmmm, a tourist, immigrant, a student—what shall you be?

Lil Girl (beaming, she declared): A Red Kite flyer, I am! (She smiled) Can't you see?

TRUTH

Is your
lifetime
ambition
non-negotiable?

Taxi

Metropolitan Museum of Art
Established: 1870
1000 Fifth Avenue New York,
NY 10028

Macy's Herald Square
Established: 1858
Location: 151 West 34th Street
New York, NY 10001

The New York Public Library (NYPL)
Established     1895
Location: 476 Fifth Avenue,
New York, New York 10018

The driver chuckled and gave her a nod.

Driver: This is now your city; wild dreams start from a bud.

Faces on large posters, once unknown now they gleam.

This is now your city, Li'l Girl, make true your dream.

Driver: So let me first take you to the Lady on the Hill.

She might have advice for that sort of unique skill.

Her gift of friendship has been trusted for years,

countless people she enlightened and she banished their fears.

Tell her your cause, don't be afraid.

The fact that you are here, you must be very brave.

## CHAPTER 3

## *A Stony Face-to-Face*

*L*ittle Girl: Good Morning, My Lady. I'm one of your
guests.
I ask of you a simple but special request.
Fly my kite from your tower, so Daddy would know,
that I arrived safely, and I miss him so.

The Lady: Well, hello, little girl, with a silly red kite.
You just got here; you must enjoy the new sites.
There are endless fashion shops, museums, and shows,
You will not miss your father even before you know.

Be independent! Excel in my many business fields.
With money your ammunition, confidence your shield.
With my power and influence, I will disciple you,
build a new self-worth, there's no time to be blue.

The Glory of Commerce
*Mercury, Hercules, Minerva*

MetLife

GRAND CENTRAL TERMINAL

Little Girl: But, Lady, I'm too homesick, overwhelmed I
   feel unwell.
I miss the love of my father and the home I know so well.

The Lady studied the girl from head to toe.
Her attention was caught to her golden pass that glows.

Lady: I see you have his golden pass in your hand,
you are free to try all amusements of my land.
I'll show you even more, if you hand me that Red Kite.
Our Federal law doesn't have a pass for that kind of flight.

The Flat Iron Building
175 5th Ave, New York, NY 10010
Opened to Public: 1902

New York advertisers would have a good grief,
to see your ancient Kite's flying little spiff.
(Mockingly)
"A little red dot, up in the air
will ruin the attractions of our Tourism Fair."

Little Girl: Oh, Lady, you now make me so sad.
My simple request isn't really that bad.
The new sights and sounds, all this is new.
Flying my Red Kite is a happy thing to do.

The Lady smiled—wise wrinkles showing her years.
But the girl saw loneliness: she was masking her tears.

# CHAPTER 4

## *A Lure, Allure, A Lie*

(The Lady's attempt to comfort the girl)

*T*he Lady: Little Girl, where are you staying?
Let me treat you out tomorrow night.
Your full satisfaction in my city is my ultimate delight.
A five-star rating, a nice blog from your pad,
the world will be amazed at the experience you had.

A full tour I will give you, all I ask you to do.
Give me that Red Kite, that's a smart thing to do.

She climbed up and down,
to clear her heart's growing chill,
as moment by moment grew,
a building sadness and fear.

(The girl thought)
*The Lady of the City desires my Red Kite?*
*Doesn't she have enough of her colored city lights?*

## CHAPTER 5

## *Grand Refuge Hotel*

*S*o the girl went home to her little hotel,
where in the midst is a grand "Living Water" well.

Are you weary?

rest

Holy Bible

**Observations of Agur**

**30** The words of Agur the son of Jakeh, *even* the prophecy: the man spake unto Ithiel, even unto Ithiel and Ucal,

2 Surely I *am* more brutish than a man, and have not the understanding of a man. Ps 73:22

26:8; Ps 2:7; Jn 3:1

5 Every w shi

**Proverbs 30:5**

**Every word of God proves true; he is a shield to those who take refuge in him.**

and the barren womb;
not filled with water;
saith not, *It is* enough.

mocketh at *his* fa-
eth to obey *his* mother,
he valley shall pick it
ung eagles shall eat it.

hree *things which* are
too wonderful for me, yea, four which
I know not: Jb 42:3

19 The way of an ea
the way of a serpent u
way o the m
an man v
wa
w h, a
mo
t
t

**PSALM**

**46** God *is* our refuge and strength, a very present help in trouble. Dt 4:7; Ps 145:18

2 Therefore will not we fear, though the earth be removed, and though the mountains be carried into the midst of the sea; Ps 18:7; 23:4

3 *Though* the waters thereof roar *and* be troubled, *though* the mountains shake with the swelling thereof. Selah. Ps 93:3-4; Jer 5:22

3 Whoso loveth wisdom rejoiceth
his father: ut he that keepeth company with lots spendeth *his* substance. Prv 15:30

4 Th dgment e
the la that
overth

5 A
b

4 *There is* a river, the streams whereof shall make glad the city of God, the holy *place* of the tabernacles of the most High. Ps 48:1; Is 60:14

5 God *is* in the midst of her; she shall not be moved: God shall help her, *and that* right early. Is 12:6; Ez 43:7

**John 7:38**

**"Whoever believes in me, as[a] the Scripture has said, 'Out of his heart will flow rivers of living water."**

le perish
happy *is*
A serva
rds: fo
not a

with a thief
; Prv 8:36
a snare:
in the
our; but
h from

ination
right in
wicked.

She took a cup to drink from her little nightstand,
splashed some water in her face with her dry weary hand.
Tears started to fall, and so she started to write—

*Dad,*
*Today I didn't fly the Red kite.*
*The Lady in the City, she took a l-o-n-g time to speak!*
*Why my little Red Kite can't fly from her tower's peak…*

Psalm 23:1-3
1 The Lord is my shepherd; I
shall not want.
2    He makes me lie down in
green pastures.
He leads me beside still
waters.[a]
3    He restores my soul.
He leads me in paths of
righteousness[b]
   for his name's sake.

Then came a knock on her "sealed" door.
A little note was passed from the slit on the floor.

*Daughter,*
*I love you. I am with you. Do not be afraid.*
*This city is passing; at home your inheritance has been laid.*
*Look closely at the Lady, and you will know.*
*Her glamour and strong foundations someday will go.*
*And in her place one day will be heaps of rocks,*
*you will be home with me, enjoying our crops.*

*Love, Dad.*

ROMANS 7:21                944

**Romans 8:37-39**
No, in all these things we are more than conquerors through him who loved us. 38 For I am sure that neither death nor life, nor angels nor rulers, nor things present nor things to come, nor powers, 39 nor height nor depth, nor anything else in all creation, will be able to separate us from the love of God in Christ Jesus our Lord.

269

**Galatians 4:3-6**
3 In the same way we also, when we were children, were enslaved to the elementary principles of the world. 4 But when the fullness of time had come, God sent forth his Son, born of woman, born under the law, 5 to redeem those who were under the law, so that we might receive adoption as sons. 6 And because you are sons, God has sent the Spirit of his Son into our hearts, crying, "Abba! Father!"

PSALM **92**
12 The righteous shall flourish like the palm tree: he shall grow like a cedar in Lebanon. Ps 52:8; Hos 14:5-6
13 Those that be planted in the house of the LORD shall flourish in the courts of our God. Ps 100:4; 135:2

*Daughter, I have loved you with an Everlasting love.*
*Dad*

And with such assurance warming her heart,
the sleepy girl got excited, "Tomorrow early I'll start!"
She climbed on her Lily 'n' Lavender bed,
with beautiful thoughts of home blooming in her head.

She wrote a note on her writing pad,
an expense report and a message to her dad.
*Dad, I bought an expensive ticket to a show.*
*The Lady said I've never been here—'till to Broadway I go.*
*Love, Daughter.*

**Psalm 91:1-4**
**My Refuge and My Fortress**

1 He who dwells in the shelter of the Most High will abide in the shadow of the Almighty.
2 I will say[a] to the Lord, "My refuge and my fortress, my God, in whom I trust."
3 For he will deliver you from the snare of the fowler and from the deadly pestilence.
4 He will cover you with his pinions, and under his wings you will find refuge; his faithfulness is a shield and buckler.

3 You return man to dust
　and say, "Return, O children of man!"[1]
4 For a thousand years in your sight
　are but as yesterday when it is past,
　or as a watch in the night.

**Ephesians 6:10-13**

The Whole Armor of God
10 Finally, be strong in the Lord and in the strength of his might. 11 Put on the whole armor of God, that you may be able to stand against the schemes of the devil. 12 For we do not wrestle against flesh and blood, but against the rulers, against the authorities, against the cosmic powers over this present darkness, against the spiritual forces of evil in the heavenly places. 13 Therefore take up the whole armor of God, that you may be able to withstand in the evil day, and having done all, to stand firm.

25 Husbands, love your wives, as Christ loved the church and gave himself up for her, 26 that he might sanctify her, having cleansed her by the washing of water with the word, 27 so that he might present the church to himself in splendor, without spot or wrinkle or any such thing, that she might be holy and without blemish.[1] 28 In the same way husbands should love their wives as their own bodies. He who loves his wife loves himself. 29 For no one ever hated his own flesh ...

yours is in heaven, and that there is no partiality with him.

*The Whole Armor of God*
10 Finally, be strong in the Lord and in the strength of his might. 11 Put on the whole armor of God, that you may be able to stand against the schemes of the devil. 12 For we do not wrestle against flesh and blood, but against the rulers, against the authorities, against the cosmic powers over this present darkness, against the spiritual forces of evil in the heavenly places. ... put on the whole armor of God, that you may be able to withstand in the evil day ... and firm. 14 Stand ... belt of truth, ... of righteous- ... having put on ... of peace. 16 In ... d of faith, with ... e flaming darts ... helmet of salva-

Dad,
I did my Accouting report.
I will be dressed appropriately tomorrow.
I am ready for the Lady.

Love and Respect,
Daughter

# CHAPTER 6

## *Broad Way, Narrow Gate*

*L*ittle Girl: Oh, Lady, what a spectacular show!
Quite extraordinary from Sunday hymns that I know.
Your shows are definitely a big highlight.
I'll never forget the magical event of tonight.

The Lady smiled proudly—a glamour alluring for years,
but the little girl saw loneliness; she was concealing her
tears.

WHERE ARE YOU HEADING?

Matthew 7:13
"Enter by the narrow gate. For the gate is wide and the way is easy that leads to destruction, and those who enter by it are many.

Matthew 7:14
For the gate is narrow and the way is hard that leads to life, and those who find it are few.

TICKETS
BROADWAY
GROUP PASS

BROADWAY

The lady flashed her long elegant hand.
And sweetly she whispered, "This could be your promise
    land.

No other city—fusion of old and new.
The neon lights that illuminate the night,
they shine brighter for you."

She smiled with a wink, what a beguiling flare!
As all night colors reflected in her endless hair.
The Lady: There comes a time, when you have to make up
    your mind,
you can't always be a "Little Girl" in your Daddy's pantomime.

James 1:14-15
"But each person is tempted when he is lured and enticed by his own desire. Then desire when it has conceived gives birth to sin, and sin when it is fully grown brings forth death. Do not be deceived, my beloved brothers. Every good gift and every perfect gift is from above, coming down from the Father of lights, with whom there is no variation or shadow due to change.

Little Girl: But Daddy is infinitely wise,
he planned this trip just for me,
to know what is in my heart and who I could be.

As I walked in your city, in my heart I could tell,
this is not the home that I desire to dwell.
So your corporate ladder, I would not climb.
To write for your city, a passion I could not find.

John 14:2-3 (KJV)

In my Father's house are many mansions: if it were not so, I would have told you.

I go to prepare a place for you.

And if I go and prepare a place for you, I will come again, and receive you unto myself; that where I am, there ye may be also.

The Lady: Give it some time, others said the same.
They shopped, wined and dined, and felt at ease with the
game.

I understand, Little Girl, all this is new—
Let New York City create a new 'you'!

Little Girl: My care for you has compelled me to speak!
For this city there's an alarm and the message is bleak.
Yes, with immense power is also a curse.
All this beauty and progress one day will disperse.

Haven't you heard of the old trumpet call?
Declaring one day judgment will fall!
Yet everyone is busy scampering, the warning they ignore.

**Rev 20:12**
And I saw the dead, great and small, standing before the throne, and books were opened. Then another book was opened, which is the book of life. And the dead were judged by what was written in the books, according to what they had done.

**Matthew 24:42-44**

Therefore, stay awake, for you do not know on what day your Lord is coming. But know this, that if the master of the house had known in what part of the night the thief was coming, he would have stayed awake and would not have let his house be broken into. Therefore you also must be ready, for the Son of Man is coming at an hour you do not expect.

**Rev 20:15**
And if anyone's name was not found written in the book of life, he was thrown into the lake of fire.

(An Indignant Lady)
Lady: Well, enough, little girl, with your morbid insights.
You are still upset; you didn't fly your Red Kite?
Fashion, fame, and promotion to extreme heights,
you can have all this; this is every girl's delight.

**Not all that glitters is Gold**

Matthew 13
*The Parable of the Hidden Treasure*
44 "The kingdom of heaven is like treasure hidden in a field, which a man found and covered up. Then in his joy he goes and sells all that he has and buys that field.

Matthew 13
*The Parable of the Pearl of Great Value*
45 "Again, the kingdom of heaven is like a merchant in search of fine pearls, 46 who, on finding one pearl of great value, went and sold all that he had and bought it.

Carnegie Hall, New York

# CHAPTER 7

## *The Biometrics*

*L*ittle Girl: Well, with respect, dear Lady, as you can see.
I am not an ordinary girl in your sophisticated city.
Dad leased this state to old kings in your land,
the time is coming; he will take it back from their hands.

(The Lady is now outraged with the Girl)
The Lady: Show me a proof, such ludicrous claim!
Can you even tell china from a real porcelain?

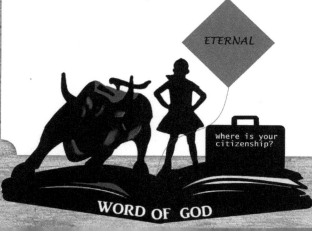

Deut 10:14
"Behold, to the Lord your God belong heaven and the heaven of heavens, the earth with all that is in it."

Isaiah 46:9-10
Remember the former things of old;
for I am God, and there is no other;
I am God, and there is none like me,
declaring the end from the beginning
and from ancient times things not yet
done, saying, 'My counsel shall stand,
and I will accomplish all my purpose,'

The Little Girl raised confidently the Red Kite in her hand,
it was actually stained by the Blood of the Lamb.

She presented to the Lady, her Gold Access Card.
Her little name was engraved in diamonds so hard.

Her pass was signed by the *Ruler Supreme*—
"To whom all nations bow down at an appointed regime."

Revelation 5:9
And they sang a new song, saying,"Worthy are you to take the scroll and to open its seals, for you were slain, and by your blood you ransomed people for God from every tribe and language and people and nation,

United Nations Headquarters, New York

The Lady grew shocked,
and touched a trembling hand to her face.
She sat down and uttered,
"When that happens, it will be a disgrace!"

The Little Girl took the Golden Pass in her bag,
and waved to the Lady, her swirling bloodstained flag.

ETERNAL

what is the
timeline
before the
deadline?

WORD OF GOD

2 Timothy 3:1-5
Godlessness in the Last Days

But understand this, that in the last days there will come times of difficulty. For people will be lovers of self, lovers of money, proud, arrogant, abusive, disobedient to their parents, ungrateful, unholy, heartless, unappeasable, slanderous, without self-control, brutal, not loving good, treacherous, reckless, swollen with conceit, lovers of pleasure rather than lovers of God, having the appearance of godliness, but denying its power.

Romans 1:32
Though they know God's righteous decree that those who practice such things deserve to die, they not only do them but give approval to those who practice them.

**Brooklyn Bridge, New York**

Little Girl: Dear Lady, before your time has begun.
This city had a Savior, who died from a distant land.
Then on the third day, He rose from the grave,
He was the fulfillment of oldest covenants made.

It is a beautiful old story, still relevant and true.
Let me tell you this story and fly this Red Kite with you.

A skeptical smile from the Lady, but the Girl held her hand.
"This story will bring redemption to your land."

ETERNAL

Is your visa
for heaven
pre-approved?

WORD OF GOD

Isaiah 53:4-6
4 Surely he has borne our griefs and carried our sorrows;
yet we esteemed him stricken, smitten by God, and afflicted.
5 But he was pierced for our transgressions; he was crushed for our
iniquities; upon him was the chastisement that brought us peace,
and with his wounds we are healed.

Empty Tomb, Jerusalem, 30-33 AD

## CHAPTER 8

## Tour Through the Heart

*T*he Lady: Well, come ride with me,
I'll take off my crown and my mask.
But this torch let me hold 'til the last spark will last.
Oh! For thinking out loud, do I have a retirement plan,
for years of holding this torch in my hand?

But this is not the time for me to whine.
Every minute of this tour, will be worth your time.
Little girl, my top five favorites, today you will see,
Why I love this city, and little girls and boys who come to
   see me.

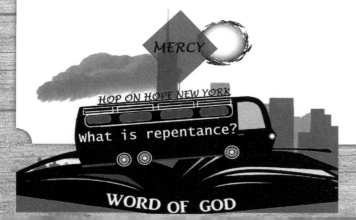

First, to my Botanical Garden fields,
of verdant flowers and trees—a peace and beauty to yield.

Or perhaps, you want to see my heart
from the standpoint of where I stand,
the Empire State building, 360-degree view to my land.

When time is ticking and chances compel you to move,
my Grand Central Station is a classic transportation groove.

Central Park Food Truck

Prov 13:20

John 15:13

Psalm 25:20-21
Oh, guard my soul,
and deliver me!
Let me not be put to
shame, for I take
refuge in you.
May integrity and
uprightness preserve
me, for I wait for
you.

Psalm 25:4
Make me to know your ways, O Lord;
teach me your paths.

Psalm 25:5
Lead me in your truth and teach me, for you are the God of my salvation;
for you I wait all the day long.

Or simply walk with a friend, get to know their heart,
with a bagel and coffee, let us walk by the Central Park.

In the middle of the changes, we try to preserve what we love,
before unexpected changes takes place from above.

Then suddenly the Lady spoke in a monotonous voice,
dark clouds and thunder accompanied her word choice.

MERCY

HOP ON HOPE NEW YORK

Are you prepared
for sudden loss
or trials?

WORD OF GOD

Psalm 49:

**Why Should I Fear in Times of Trouble?**

5 Why should I fear in times of trouble,
   when the iniquity of those who cheat me
surrounds me,
6 those who trust in their wealth
   and boast of the abundance of their riches?
7 Truly no man can ransom another,
   or give to God the price of his life,
8 for the ransom of their life is costly
   and can never suffice,
9 that he should live on forever
   and never see the pit.

10 For he sees that even the wise die;
   the fool and the stupid alike must perish
   and leave their wealth to others.
11 Their graves are their homes forever,[a]
   their dwelling places to all generations,
   though they called lands by their own names.
12 Man in his pomp will not remain;
   he is like the beasts that perish.

17 For when he dies he will carry nothing away;
   his glory will not go down after him.
18 For though, while he lives, he counts himself
blessed
   —and though you get praise when you do well
for yourself—
19 his soul will go to the generation of his fathers,
   who will never again see light.
20 Man in his pomp yet without understanding is
like the beasts that perish.

VIJAYASHANKER PARAMSOTHY          SANDRA LEE WRIGHT
GEIS     MICHAEL WILLIAM LOMAX          THERESA
AMUEL GARDNER     JOHN ADAM LARSON
9/11 Memorial & Museum New York

This One World Trade Center is a solemn place to see,
it is a bittersweet reminder of two dearest friends to me.
For I have a traumatic story to tell,
the day my best friends the Twin Sisters they fell.

Oh, Little Girl, I just stood there and watched,
with their beauty and power—attacked they collapsed.

Ecclesiastes 3

**A Time for Everything**

3 For everything there is a season, and a
time for every matter under heaven:
2 a time to be born, and a time to die;
a time to plant, and a time to pluck up
what is planted;
3 a time to kill, and a time to heal; a time
to break down, and a time to build up;
4 a time to weep, and a time to laugh;
a time to mourn, and a time to dance;
5 a time to cast away stones, and a time to
gather stones together;
a time to embrace, and a time to refrain
from embracing;
6 a time to seek, and a time to lose;
a time to keep, and a time to cast away;
7 a time to tear, and a time to sew;
a time to keep silence, and a time to speak;

Ecclesiastes 3: 11
He has made everything beautiful in its time.
Also, he has put eternity into man's heart,
yet so that he cannot find out what God has
done from the beginning to the end.

New York Botanical
Garden, Bronx New York

Empire Estate
Building, New York

Grand Central
Terminal, New York

If I am truly free, and my feet could run,
I would have tried my best to stop the enemies at hand.
But I stood my ground and held tight to this role,
I am a symbol of freedom and opportunity,
this is a man-made goal.

So silently that day, I cried to the God who can save!
I was crushed and helpless—3,000 went down to the grave.

MERCY

HOP ON HOPE NEW YORK

What awaits me in future eternity?

WORD OF GOD

Romans 9:19c-23
"For who can resist his will?"
20 But who are you, O man, to answer back to God? Will what is molded say to its molder, "Why have you made me like this?"
21 Has the potter no right over the clay, to make out of the same lump one vessel for honorable use and another for dishonorable use?
22 What if God, desiring to show his wrath and to make known his power, has endured with much patience vessels of wrath prepared for destruction,
23 in order to make known the riches of his glory for vessels of mercy, which he has prepared beforehand for glory.

In Loving Memory
of
The Twin Towers

World Trade Ctr 1 - 1,368 ft
World Trade Ctr 2 - 1,362 ft
Status: Destroyed
Active Years 1973-2001
Lower Manhattan,
New York City

RIP
John 5:28-29

RIP
John 11:25

Twin Towers, Lower Manhattan,
New York - 1973-2001

# CHAPTER 9

## *A Solemn Rejoicing*

𝓛ittle Girl: At a glance, people think
you have a heart that can't bleed.
But you are wise and caring, hear my story, I plead.

I cannot trade Red Kite flying, for another career,
for the greater need is the Gospel for your people to hear.

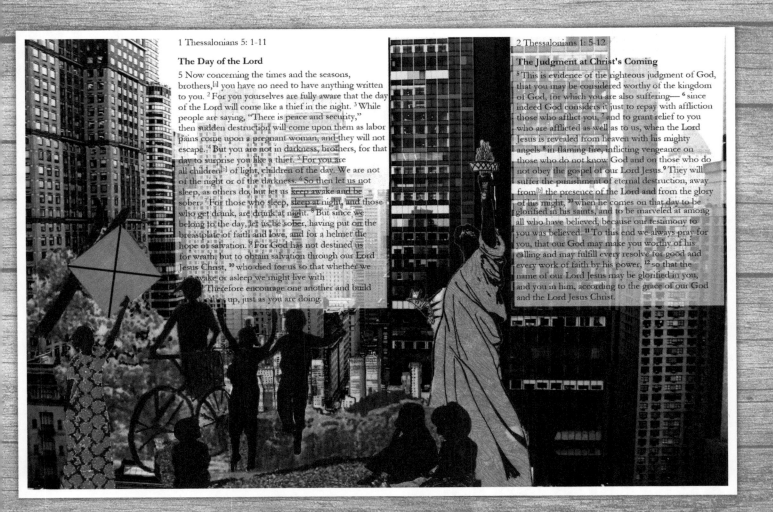

1 Thessalonians 5: 1–11

**The Day of the Lord**

5 Now concerning the times and the seasons, brothers,[a] you have no need to have anything written to you. 2 For you yourselves are fully aware that the day of the Lord will come like a thief in the night. 3 While people are saying, "There is peace and security," then sudden destruction will come upon them as labor pains come upon a pregnant woman, and they will not escape. 4 But you are not in darkness, brothers, for that day to surprise you like a thief. 5 For you are all children[b] of light, children of the day. We are not of the night or of the darkness. 6 So then let us not sleep, as others do, but let us keep awake and be sober. 7 For those who sleep, sleep at night, and those who get drunk, are drunk at night. 8 But since we belong to the day, let us be sober, having put on the breastplate of faith and love, and for a helmet the hope of salvation. 9 For God has not destined us for wrath, but to obtain salvation through our Lord Jesus Christ, 10 who died for us so that whether we are awake or asleep we might live with ... 11 Therefore encourage one another and build one another up, just as you are doing.

2 Thessalonians 1: 5-12

**The Judgment at Christ's Coming**

5 This is evidence of the righteous judgment of God, that you may be considered worthy of the kingdom of God, for which you are also suffering— 6 since indeed God considers it just to repay with affliction those who afflict you, 7 and to grant relief to you who are afflicted as well as to us, when the Lord Jesus is revealed from heaven with his mighty angels 8 in flaming fire, inflicting vengeance on those who do not know God and on those who do not obey the gospel of our Lord Jesus. 9 They will suffer the punishment of eternal destruction, away from[b] the presence of the Lord and from the glory of his might, 10 when he comes on that day to be glorified in his saints, and to be marveled at among all who have believed, because our testimony to you was believed. 11 To this end we always pray for you, that our God may make you worthy of his calling and may fulfill every resolve for good and every work of faith by his power, 12 so that the name of our Lord Jesus may be glorified in you, and you in him, according to the grace of our God and the Lord Jesus Christ.

There is Good News for all people in the land.
They are privileged and redeemed by the Blood of the
  Lamb.
While they toil so hard in this city to please,
neon gods who can't save or give justice and peace.

All slavery and oppression in all of the lands,
He took it upon Him, as they nailed His hands.
Dying, He looked up to His Father above.
And said, "It is finished—they are redeemed out of love."

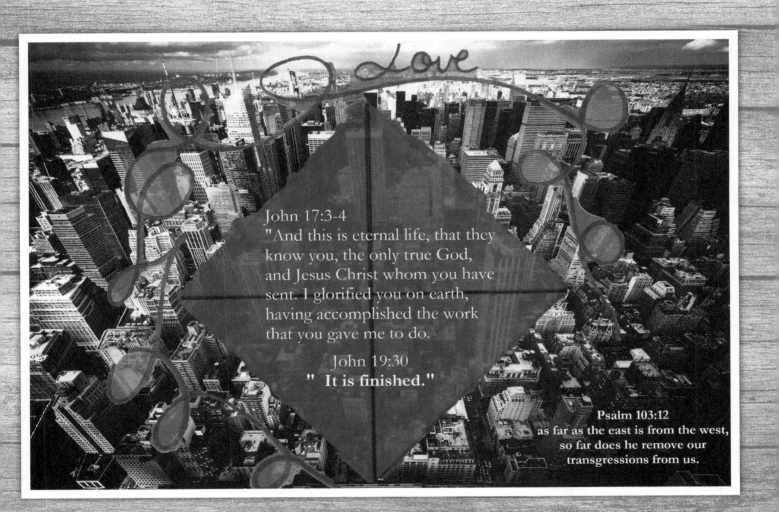

*Love*

John 17:3-4
"And this is eternal life, that they
know you, the only true God,
and Jesus Christ whom you have
sent. I glorified you on earth,
having accomplished the work
that you gave me to do.

John 19:30
" It is finished."

Psalm 103:12
as far as the east is from the west,
so far does he remove our
transgressions from us.

A great temple was torn as He spoke His last,
affirming His Sonship; they stood there aghast.
And on the third day, He rose from the grave,
the event fulfilled; oldest covenants made.

And Lady, these times are now moving too fast,
to fulfill His Second Coming, as prophesied from the past.
Not as a meek Lamb, who was slaughtered for sin,
but as Ruler and Judge, His forever reign will begin.

St. Patrick's Cathedral, New York

## Matthew 27

### Jesus Is Mocked

27 Then the soldiers of the governor took [Jesus] to the governor's headquarters,[d] and gathered the whole battalion[e] before him. And they stripped him and put a scarlet robe on him, and twisting together a crown of thorns, they put it on his head and put a reed in his right hand. And kneeling before him they mocked him, saying, "Hail, King of the Jews!" And they spit on him and took the reed and struck him on the head. And when they had mocked him, they stripped him of the robe and put his own clothes on him and led him away to crucify him.

...a man of ...compelled this ...when they came ...ch means Place ...wine to drink, ...tasted it, he would ...had crucified ...among them by ...down and kept ...over his head ...him, which read, ..."This is Jesus, the King of the Jews." 38 Then ...with him, one on ...9 And those who ...their heads 40 ...destroy the temple ...save yourself! If you ...down from the ...priests, with the ...him, saying, 42 ...save himself. ...come ...and we will ...God; let ...desires him. ...God.'"

### The Death of Jesus

45 Now from the sixth hour[f] there was darkness over all the land[g] until the ninth hour.[h] 46 And about the ninth hour Jesus cried out with a loud voice, saying, "Eli, Eli, lema sabachthani?" that is, "My God, my God, why have you forsaken me?" 47 And some of the bystanders, hearing it, said, "This man is calling Elijah." 48 And one of them at once ran and took a sponge, filled it with sour wine, and put it on a reed and gave it to him to drink. 49 But the others said, "Wait, let us see whether Elijah will come to save him." 50 And Jesus cried out again with a loud voice and yielded up his spirit.

51 And behold, the curtain of the temple was torn in two, from top to bottom. And the earth shook, and the rocks were split. 52 The tombs also were opened. And many bodies of the saints who had fallen asleep were raised, 53 and coming out of the tombs after his resurrection they went into the holy city and appeared to many. 54 When the centurion and those who were with him, keeping watch over Jesus, saw the earthquake and what took place, they were filled with awe and said, "Truly this was the Son[i] of God!"

55 There were also many women there, looking on from a distance, who had followed Jesus from Galilee, ministering to him, 56 among whom were Mary Magdalene and Mary the mother of James and Joseph and the mother of the sons of Zebedee.

### Jesus Is Buried

57 When it was evening, there came a rich man from Arimathea, named Joseph, who also was a disciple of Jesus. 58 He went to Pilate and asked for the body of Jesus. Then Pilate ordered it to be given to him. 59 And Joseph took the body and wrapped it in a clean linen shroud 60 and laid it in his own new tomb, which he had cut in the rock. And he rolled a great stone to the entrance of the tomb and went away. 61 Mary Magdalene and the other Mary were there, sitting opposite the tomb.

### The Guard at the Tomb

64 Therefore order the tomb to be made secure until the third day, lest his disciples go and steal him away and tell the people, 'He has risen from the dead,' and the last fraud will be worse than the first." 65 Pilate said to them, "You have a guard[j] of soldiers. Go, make it as secure as you can." 66 So they went and made the tomb secure by sealing the stone and setting a guard.

There is an important message from Dad.
About that retirement plan, you thought you never had.

One day you can put down your torch, crown, and robe.
My Father will recreate the face of this globe.

## Romans 7

21 So I find it to be a law that when I want to do right, evil lies close at hand. For I delight in the law of God, in my inner being, but I see in my members another law waging war against the law of my mind and making me captive to the law of sin that dwells in my members. Wretched man that I am! Who will deliver me from this body of death? 25 Thanks be to God through Jesus Christ our Lord! So then, I myself serve the law of God with my mind, but with my flesh I serve the law of sin.

## Romans 8
## Life in the Spirit

8 There is therefore now no condemnation for those who are in Christ Jesus. For the law of the Spirit of life has set you free in Christ Jesus from the law of sin and death. 3 For God has done what the law, weakened by the flesh, could not do. By sending his own Son in the likeness of sinful flesh and for sin, he condemned sin in the flesh, in order that the righteous requirement of the law might be fulfilled in us, who walk not according to the flesh but according to the Spirit. For those who live according to the flesh set their minds on the things of the flesh, but those who live according to the Spirit set their minds on the things of the Spirit. For to set the mind on the flesh is death, but to set the mind on the Spirit is life and peace. 7 For the mind that is set on the flesh is hostile to God, for it does not submit to God's law; indeed, it cannot. 8 Those who are in the flesh cannot please God.

9 You, however, are not in the flesh but in the Spirit, if in fact the Spirit of God dwells in you. Anyone who does not have the Spirit of Christ does not belong to him. 10 But if Christ is in you, although the body is dead because of sin, the Spirit is life because of righteousness. 11 If the Spirit of him who raised Jesus from the dead dwells in you, he who raised Christ Jesus[d] from the dead will also give life to your mortal bodies through his Spirit who dwells in you.

## Future Glory

18 For I consider that the sufferings of this present time are not worth comparing with the glory that is to be revealed to us. 19 For the creation waits with eager longing for the revealing of the sons of God. 20 For the creation was subjected to futility, not willingly, but because of him who subjected it, in hope 21 that the creation itself will be set free from its bondage to corruption and obtain the freedom of the glory of the children of God. 22 For we know that the whole creation has been groaning together in the pains of childbirth until now. 23 And not only the creation, but we ourselves, who have the firstfruits of the Spirit, groan inwardly as we wait eagerly for adoption as sons, the redemption of our bodies. For in this hope we were saved. Now hope that is seen is not hope. For who hopes for what he sees? 25 But if we hope for what we do not see, we wait for it with patience.

## God's Everlasting Love

31 What then shall we say to these things? If God is for us, who can be against us? 32 He who did not spare his own Son but gave him up for us all, how will he not also with him graciously give us all things? 33 Who shall bring any charge against God's elect? It is God who justifies. 34 Who is to condemn? Christ Jesus is the one who died—more than that, who was raised—who is at the right hand of God, who indeed is interceding for us.[j] 35 Who shall separate us from the love of Christ? Shall tribulation, or distress, or persecution, or famine, or nakedness, or danger, or sword? As it is written,

"For your sake we are being killed all the day long; we are regarded as sheep to be slaughtered."

37 No, in all these things we are more than conquerors through him who loved us. 38 For I am sure that neither death nor life, nor angels nor rulers, nor things present nor things to come, nor powers, 39 nor height nor depth, nor anything else in all creation, will be able to separate us from the love of God in Christ Jesus our Lord.

Bethesda Fountain, Central Park, NY

## CHAPTER 10

## Melt My Heart of Stone

The Little Girl wiped away tears from her eyes,
as the Lady exhaled a long deep sigh.
She asked the Lady, if she can lift her high,
some truths are meant said straight in the eye.

The Little Girl touched the Lady's stony face.
God is Righteous and Holy; He gives faith and grace.

Gospel
of
Jesus Christ

Do you know Him who
truly loves you?

The Power of The Word of God

### God's Righteous Judgment

2 Therefore you have no excuse, O man, every one of you who judges. For in passing judgment on another you condemn yourself, because you, the judge, practice the very same things. 2 We know that the judgment of God rightly falls on those who practice such things. 3 Do you suppose, O man—you who judge those who practice such things and yet do them yourself—that you will escape the judgment of God? 4 Or do you presume on the riches of his kindness and forbearance and patience, not knowing that God's kindness is meant to lead you to repentance? 5 But because of your hard and impenitent heart you are storing up wrath for yourself on the day of wrath when God's righteous judgment will be revealed. 6 He will render to each one according to his works: 7 to those who by patience in well-doing seek for glory and honor and immortality, he will give eternal life; 8 but for those who are self-seeking and do not obey the truth, but obey unrighteousness, there will be wrath and fury.

### God's Righteousness Upheld

4 Let God be true though every one were a liar, as it is written,

"That you may be justified in your words, and prevail when you are judged."

5 But if our unrighteousness serves to show the righteousness of God, what shall we say? That God is unrighteous to inflict wrath on us? (I speak in a human way.) 6 By no means! For then how could God judge the world? 7 But if through my lie God's truth abounds to his glory, why am I still being condemned as a sinner? 8 And why not do evil that good may come?—as some people slanderously charge us with saying. Their condemnation is just.

### No One Is Righteous

9 What then? Are we Jews any better off?[b] No, not at all. For we have already charged that all, both Jews and Greeks, are under sin, 10 as it is written:

"None is righteous, no, not one;
11 no one understands;
   no one seeks for God.
12 All have turned aside;
together they have become worthless;
   no one does good,
   not even one."

### The Righteousness of God Through Faith

21 But now the righteousness of God has been manifested apart from the law, although the Law and the Prophets bear witness to it— 22 the righteousness of God through faith in Jesus Christ for all who believe. For there is no distinction: 23 for all have sinned and fall short of the glory of God, 24 and are justified by his grace as a gift, through the redemption that is in Christ Jesus, 25 whom God put forward as a propitiation by his blood, to be received by faith. This was to show God's righteousness, because in his divine forbearance he had passed over former sins. 26 It was to show his righteousness at the present time, so that he might be just and the justifier of the one who has faith in Jesus. 27 Then what becomes of our boasting? It is excluded. By what kind of law? By a law of works? No, but by the law of faith. 28 For we hold that one is justified by faith apart from works of the law. 29 Or is God the God of Jews only? Is he not the God of Gentiles also? Yes, of Gentiles also, 30 since God is one— who will justify the circumcised by faith and the uncircumcised through faith. 31 Do we then overthrow the law by this faith? By no means! On the contrary, we uphold the law.

The Lady: I don't have a Daddy, it's hard to fully empathize.
From hundred hands I was formed, can't you see it with
    your eyes?
But for their hope, I ask for faith—may my heart be made
    new,
you are so little, but you have courage, because your passion
    is true.

Little Girl: Dear Lady, your words a miracle to hear.
Are you now my true friend, may your yes be made clear?

The Lady smiled, a radiance never seen for years!
The Little Girl saw no longer any traces of tears.

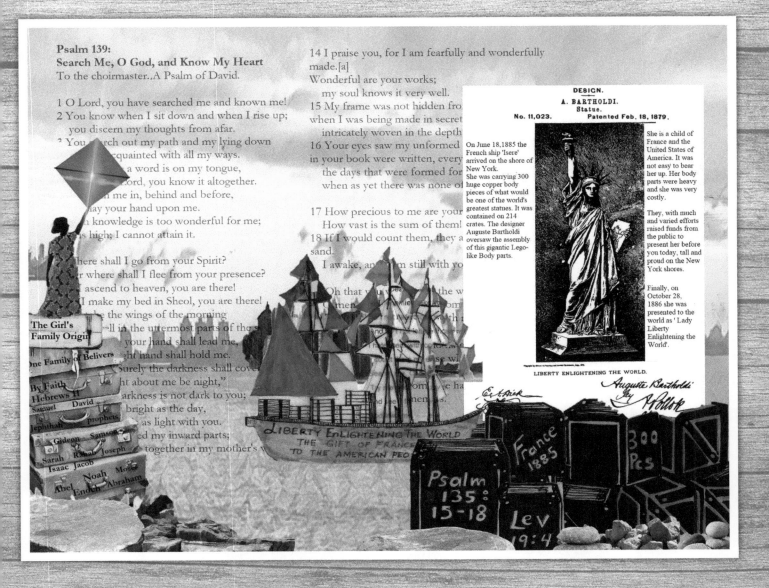

Psalm 139:
**Search Me, O God, and Know My Heart**
To the choirmaster..A Psalm of David.

1 O Lord, you have searched me and known me!
2 You know when I sit down and when I rise up;
   you discern my thoughts from afar.
3 You search out my path and my lying down
   and are acquainted with all my ways.
4 Even before a word is on my tongue,
   behold, O Lord, you know it altogether.
5 You hem me in, behind and before,
   and lay your hand upon me.
6 Such knowledge is too wonderful for me;
   it is high; I cannot attain it.

7 Where shall I go from your Spirit?
   Or where shall I flee from your presence?
8 If I ascend to heaven, you are there!
   If I make my bed in Sheol, you are there!
9 If I take the wings of the morning
   and dwell in the uttermost parts of the sea,
10 even there your hand shall lead me,
   and your right hand shall hold me.
11 If I say, "Surely the darkness shall cover me,
   and the light about me be night,"
12 even the darkness is not dark to you;
   the night is bright as the day,
   for darkness is as light with you.
13 For you formed my inward parts;
   you knitted me together in my mother's womb.

14 I praise you, for I am fearfully and wonderfully made.[a]
Wonderful are your works;
   my soul knows it very well.
15 My frame was not hidden from you,
when I was being made in secret,
   intricately woven in the depths of the earth.
16 Your eyes saw my unformed substance;
in your book were written, every one of them,
   the days that were formed for me,
   when as yet there was none of them.

17 How precious to me are your thoughts, O God!
   How vast is the sum of them!
18 If I would count them, they are more than the sand.
   I awake, and I am still with you.

The Girl's Family Origin

One Family of Belivers
By Faith
Hebrews 11
Samuel   David
Jephthah   prophets
Gideon   Samson
Sarah   Rahab   Joseph
Isaac   Jacob
Abel   Noah   Moses
Enoch   Abraham

LIBERTY ENLIGHTENING THE WORLD
THE GIFT OF FRANCE
TO THE AMERICAN PEOPLE

Psalm 135: 15-18
France 1885
300 Pcs
Lev 19:4

DESIGN.
A. BARTHOLDI.
Statue.
No. 11,023.       Patented Feb. 18, 1879.

On June 18,1885 the French ship 'Isere' arrived on the shore of New York.
She was carrying 300 huge copper body pieces of what would be one of the world's greatest statues. It was contained on 214 crates. The designer Auguste Bartholdi oversaw the assembly of this gigantic Lego-like Body parts.

She is a child of France and the United States of America. It was not easy to bear her up. Her body parts were heavy and she was very costly.

They, with much and varied efforts raised funds from the public to present her before you today, tall and proud on the New York shores.

Finally, on October 28, 1886 she was presented to the world as ' Lady Liberty Enlightening the World'.

LIBERTY ENLIGHTENING THE WORLD.

The Lady arranged her crown with seven rays on her hair.
The Little Girl threw flowers for her up in the air!

The Lady she smiled, butterfly kisses she blew.
Making elegant cloud flowers in the sky so blue.

The Lady: And when your Daddy renews the face of this
land.
Can He do me a favor with His Mighty hand?
Little Girl, I'm big and stony, and all I want is to be,
with little arms to hug the girl who shared the Gospel to me.

## 2 Corinthians 1

### God of All Comfort

3 Blessed be the God and Father of our Lord Jesus Christ, the Father of mercies and God of all comfort, 4 who comforts us in all our affliction, so that we may be able to comfort those who are in any affliction, with the comfort with which we ourselves are comforted by God. 5 For as we share abundantly in Christ's sufferings, so through Christ we share abundantly in comfort too.[a] 6 If we are afflicted, it is for your comfort and salvation; and if we are comforted, it is for your comfort, which you experience when you patiently endure the same sufferings that we suffer. 7 Our hope for you is unshaken, for we know that as you share in our sufferings, you will also share in our comfort.

### Paul's Change of

12 For our boast is
conscience, that we
simplicity[c] and go
wisdom but by the
you. 13 For

### 2 Corinthians 2

### Triumph in Christ

14 But thanks be to God, who in Christ always
triumphal procession, and through us spreads
of the knowledge of him everywhere.
15 For we are the aroma of Christ to God am
who are being saved and among those who
to one a fragrance from death to death
things? 17 For we are not, like so m
word, but as men of sincerity, as comm
the sight of God we speak in Christ.

### 2 Corinthians 3

### Ministers of the New Covenant

3 Are we beginning to commend ourselves
need, as some do, letters of recommen
from you or you yourselves are our letter
written on our[a] heart
3 And you sh
ed by us, writt

### 2 Cor 4

### The Light of the Gospel

1.Therefore, having this ministry by the mercy of God,[a] we do not lose heart. 2 But we have renounced disgra... underhanded ways. We refuse to practice[b] cu... to tamper with God's word, but by the open...ment of the truth we would commend ourselve...to everyone's conscience in the ...ht of God. 3 A...even if our gospel is veiled, it is ...to those ...are perishing. 4 In their case the ...d has blinded the minds of the ...o keep them from seeing the light of the ...e glory of Christ, who is the image of ...or what we proclaim is not ourselves, but ...Christ as Lord, with ourselves as your ...ants[c] for Jesus' sake. 6 For God, who said, "Let ...shine out of darkness" has shone in our hearts ...ve the light...wledge of the glory of God ...e face o...

...sure in J...
...we do n...
...nmanna...
...whe...
...al...

Bryant Park, New York

Little Girl: Oh hush, hush, Lady! You again make me cry.
Pretty please, it is time for our Red Kite to fly.

So the Lady took her up to an airy porch on her torch,
then she sang in her most b-e-a-u-t-i-f-u-l voice!
**"Fly, Red Kite, of course!"**

## Philippians 1

### Thanksgiving and Prayer

3 I thank my God in all my remembrance of you, always in every prayer of mine for you all making my prayer with joy, 5 because of your partnership in the gospel from the first day until now. 6 And I am sure of this, that he who began a good work in you will bring it to completion at the day of Jesus Christ. 7 It is right for me to feel this way about you all, because I hold you in my heart, for you are all partakers with me of grace,[d] both in my imprisonment and in the defense and confirmation of the gospel. 8 For God is my witness, how I yearn for you all with the affection of Christ Jesus. 9 And it is my prayer that your love may abound more and more, with knowledge and all discernment, 10 so that you may approve what is excellent, and so be pure and blameless for the day of Christ, 11 filled with the fruit of righteousness that comes through Jesus Christ, to the glory and praise of God.

### The Advance of the Gospel

12 I want you to know, brothers,[e] that what has happened to me has really served to advance the gospel, 13 so that it has become known throughout the whole imperial guard[f] and to all the rest that my imprisonment is for Christ. 14 And most of the brothers, having become confident in the Lord by my imprisonment, are much more bold to speak the word[g] without fear.

15 Some indeed preach Christ from envy and rivalry, but others from good will. 16 The latter do it out of love, knowing that I am put here for the defense of the gospel. 17 The former proclaim Christ out of selfish ambition, not sincerely but thinking to afflict me in my imprisonment. 18 What then? Only that in every way, whether in pretense or in truth, Christ is proclaimed, and in that I rejoice.

### To Live Is Christ

Yes, and I will rejoice, 19 for I know that through your prayers and the help of the Spirit of Jesus Christ this will turn out for my deliverance, 20 as it is my eager expectation and hope that I will not be at all ashamed, but that with full courage now as always Christ will be honored in my body, whether by life or by death. 21 For to me to live is Christ, and to die is gain. 22 If I am to live in the flesh, that means fruitful labor for me. Yet which I shall choose I cannot tell. 23 I am hard pressed between the two. My desire is to depart and be with Christ, for that is far better. 24 But to remain in the flesh is more necessary on your account.

### To Live Is Christ

Yes, and I will rejoice, 19 for I know that through your prayers and the help of the Spirit of Jesus Christ this will turn out for my deliverance, 20 as it is my eager expectation and hope that I will not be at all ashamed, but that with full courage now as always Christ will be honored in my body, whether by life or by death. 21 For to me to live is Christ, and to die is gain. 22 If I am to live in the flesh, that means fruitful labor for me. Yet which I shall choose I cannot tell. 23 I am hard pressed between the two. My desire is to depart and be with Christ, for that is far better. 24 But to remain in the flesh is more necessary on your account. 25 Convinced of this, I know that I will remain and continue with you all, for your progress and joy in the faith, 26 so that in me you may have ample cause to glory in Christ Jesus, because of my coming to you again.

27 Only let your manner of life be worthy of the gospel of Christ, so that whether I come and see you or am absent, I may hear of you that you are standing firm in one spirit, with one mind striving side by side for the faith of the gospel, 28 and not frightened in anything by your opponents. This is a clear sign to them of their destruction, but of your salvation, and that from God. 29 For it has been granted to you that for the sake of Christ you should not only believe in him but also suffer for his sake, 30 engaged in the same conflict that you saw I had and now hear that I still have.

## Philippians 2
### Lights in the World

12 Therefore, my beloved, as you have always obeyed, so now, not only as in my presence but much more in my absence, work out your own salvation with fear and trembling, 13 for it is God who works in you, both to will and to work for his good pleasure.

## Philippians 3:
### Straining Toward the Goal

12 Not that I have already obtained this or am already perfect, but I press on to make it my own, because Christ Jesus has made me his own. 13 Brothers, I do not consider that I have made it my own. But one thing I do: forgetting what lies behind and straining forward to what lies ahead, 14 I press on toward the goal for the prize of the upward call of God in Christ Jesus. 15 Let those of us who are mature think this way, and if in anything you think otherwise, God will reveal that also to you. 16 Only let us hold true to what we have attained.

So that afternoon, the Lady and the Little Girl,
shared a memory more precious
than all the worlds diamonds and pearls.

As the glowing sunset turned slowly to night,
her Daddy from the mountains saw the Red Kite.
It waved a merciful red on the city's fading light.
He was pleased with the choice of His daughter's delight.

*The end is just the beginning…*

## 1 Peter 1

### Born Again to a Living Hope

3 Blessed be the God and Father of our Lord Jesus Christ! According to his great mercy, he has caused us to be born again to a living hope through the resurrection of Jesus Christ from the dead, 4 to an inheritance that is imperishable, undefiled, and unfading, kept in heaven for you, 5 who by God's power are being guarded through faith for a salvation ready to be revealed in the last time. 6 In this you rejoice, though now for a little while, if necessary, you have been grieved by various trials, 7 so that the tested genuineness of your faith—more precious than gold that perishes though it is tested by fire—may be found to result in praise and glory and honor at the revelation of Jesus Christ. 8 Though you have not seen him, you love him. Though you do not now see him, you believe in him and rejoice with joy that is inexpressible and filled with glory, 9 obtaining the outcome of your faith, the salvation of your souls.

### Called to Be Holy

13 Therefore, preparing your minds for action, [b] and being sober-minded, set your hope fully on the grace that will be brought to you at the revelation of Jesus Christ. 14 As obedient children, do not be conformed to the passions of your former ignorance, 15 but as he who called you is holy, you also be holy in all your conduct, 16 since it is written, "You shall be holy, for I am holy." 17 And if you call on him as Father who judges impartially according to each one's deeds, conduct yourselves with fear throughout the time of your exile, 18 knowing that you were ransomed from the futile ways inherited from your forefathers, not with perishable things such as silver or gold, 19 but with the precious blood of Christ, like that of a lamb without blemish or spot.

## 1 Peter 3:

### Suffering for Righteousness' Sake

8 Finally, all of you, have unity of mind, sympathy, brotherly love, a tender heart, and a humble mind. 9 Do not repay evil for evil or reviling for reviling, but on the contrary, bless, for to this you were called, that you may obtain a blessing. 10 For "Whoever desires to love life
  and see good days,
  let him keep his tongue from evil
  and his lips from speaking deceit;
11 let him turn away from evil and do good;
  let him seek peace and pursue it.
12 For the eyes of the Lord are on the righteous,
  and his ears are open to their prayer.
But the face of the Lord is against those who do evil."

## 1 Peter 5

### Shepherd the Flock of God

6 Humble yourselves, therefore, under the mighty hand of God so that at the proper time he may exalt you, 7 casting all your anxieties on him, because he cares for you. 8 Be sober-minded; be watchful. Your adversary the devil prowls around like a roaring lion, seeking someone to devour. 9 Resist him, firm in your faith, knowing that the same kinds of suffering are being experienced by your brotherhood throughout the world. 10 And after you have suffered a little while, the God of all grace, who has called you to his eternal glory in Christ, will himself restore, confirm, strengthen, and establish you. 11 To him be the dominion forever and ever. Amen.

# THE
# LADY
## AND
# GIRL
### WITH A
# *Red Kite*

A. Guevara

## Pledge to My Bible

This is my Bible.
It is God's Holy Word.
It is a lamp unto my feet
and a light unto my path.
It tells me who I am,
who I can become,
and where I am going.

It renews my mind,
it changes my heart,
it refreshes my soul.
It is my daily bread.

By faith I will believe its promises,
obey its commandments,
and honor its principles in my life.

With the Bible as my guide,
I will walk by faith and not by sight.

_Resource copied from:
Katipunan Bible Baptist Church
Katipunan St. Cebu City, Philippines.
07.01.2013

You have chosen the roughest road, but it leads straight to the hilltops.

–John Bunyan

# Chapter 1
## These Biblical truths shaped my train of thoughts, secured me with love, faith and endless hopes.

### What is in your heart?

"Hear, O Israel: The Lord our God, the Lord is one. You shall love the Lord your God with all your heart and with all your soul and with all your might. And these words that I command you today shall be on your heart. You shall teach them diligently to your children, and shall talk of them when you sit in your house, and when you walk by the way, and when you lie down, and when you rise. You shall bind them as a sign on your hand, and they shall be as frontlets between your eyes. You shall write them on the doorposts of your house and on your gates.

*DEUTERONOMY 6:4-9*

**What are you often thinking about?**

This Book of the Law shall not depart from your mouth,
but you shall meditate on it day and night, so that you may
be careful to do according to all that is written in it.

*JOSHUA 1:8 ESV*

and....

Finally, brethren, whatsoever things are true, whatsoever things
are honest, whatsoever things are just, whatsoever things are pure,
whatsoever things are lovely, whatsoever things are of good report; if
there be any virtue, and if there be any praise, think on these things.
Those things, which ye have both learned, and received, and heard,
and seen in me, do: and the God of peace shall be with you.

*PHILIPPIANS 4:8-9 KJV*

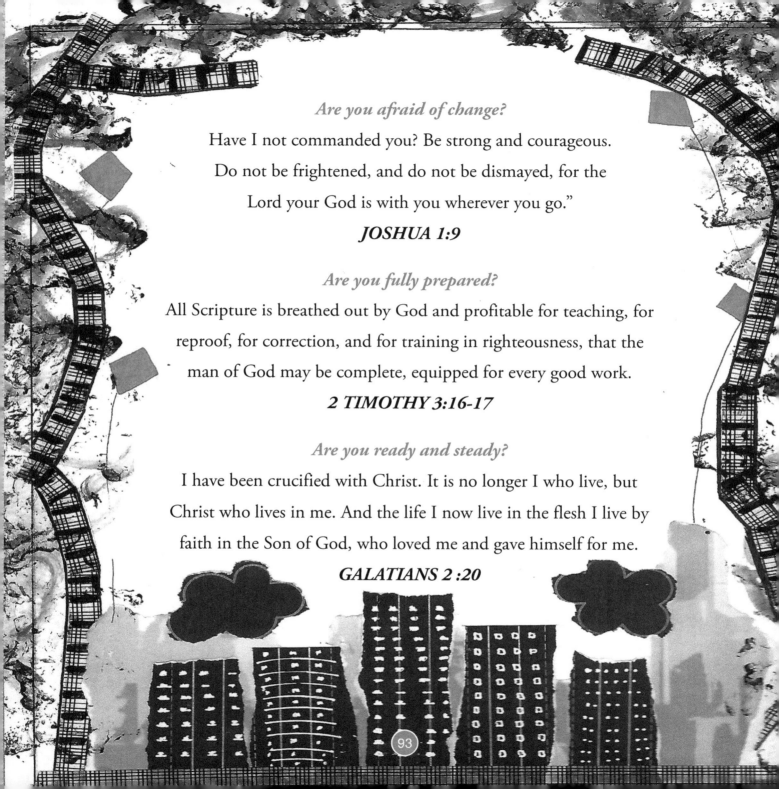

*Are you afraid of change?*

Have I not commanded you? Be strong and courageous.
Do not be frightened, and do not be dismayed, for the
Lord your God is with you wherever you go."

**JOSHUA 1:9**

*Are you fully prepared?*

All Scripture is breathed out by God and profitable for teaching, for
reproof, for correction, and for training in righteousness, that the
man of God may be complete, equipped for every good work.

**2 TIMOTHY 3:16-17**

*Are you ready and steady?*

I have been crucified with Christ. It is no longer I who live, but
Christ who lives in me. And the life I now live in the flesh I live by
faith in the Son of God, who loved me and gave himself for me.

**GALATIANS 2 :20**

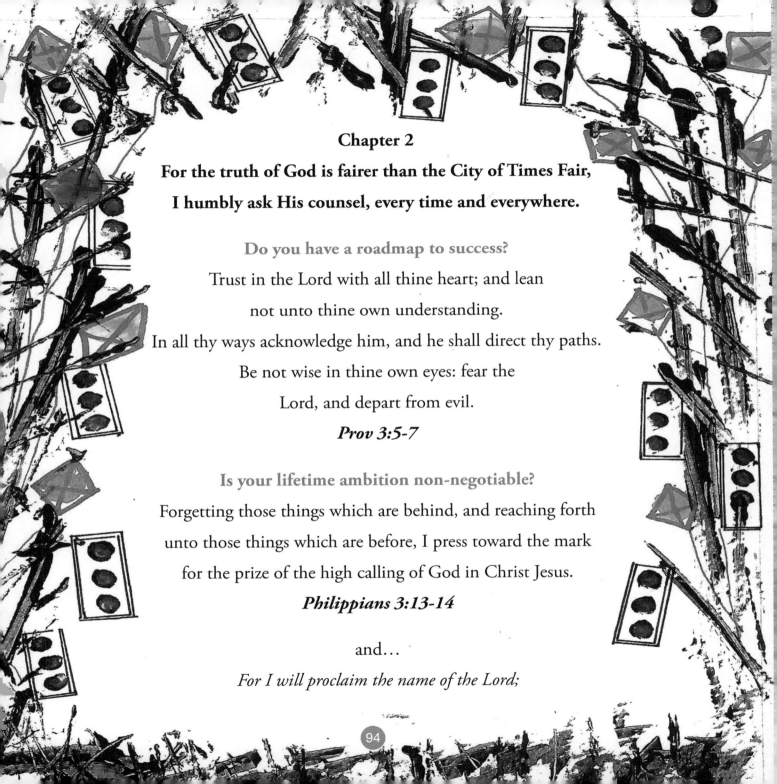

## Chapter 2

**For the truth of God is fairer than the City of Times Fair,
I humbly ask His counsel, every time and everywhere.**

Do you have a roadmap to success?

Trust in the Lord with all thine heart; and lean

not unto thine own understanding.

In all thy ways acknowledge him, and he shall direct thy paths.

Be not wise in thine own eyes: fear the

Lord, and depart from evil.

***Prov 3:5-7***

Is your lifetime ambition non-negotiable?

Forgetting those things which are behind, and reaching forth

unto those things which are before, I press toward the mark

for the prize of the high calling of God in Christ Jesus.

***Philippians 3:13-14***

and…

*For I will proclaim the name of the Lord;*

*ascribe greatness to our God!*
*"The Rock, his work is perfect,*
*for all his ways are justice.*
*A God of faithfulness and without iniquity,*
*just and upright is he.*
**Deuteronomy 32:3-4**

*Do you have trustworthy role models?*

By faith we understand that the universe was created by the word of God, so that what is seen was not made out of things that are visible. **By faith Abraham obeyed** when he was called to go out to a place that he was to receive as an inheritance. And he went out, not knowing where he was going. By faith he went to live in the land of promise, as in a foreign land, living in tents with Isaac and Jacob, heirs with him of the same promise. ***For he was looking forward to the city that has foundations, whose designer and builder is God.*** By faith Sarah herself received power to conceive, even when she

was past the age, since she considered him faithful who had promised. Therefore, from one man, and him as good as dead, were born descendants as many as the stars of heaven and as many as the innumerable grains of sand by the seashore. These all died in faith, not having received the things promised, but having seen them and greeted them from afar, and *having acknowledged that they were strangers and exiles on the earth.* For people who speak thus make it clear that they are seeking a homeland. If they had been thinking of that land from which they had gone out, they would have had opportunity to return. But as it is, *they desire a better country, that is, a heavenly one. Therefore, God is not ashamed to be called their God, for he has prepared for them a city.*
*Hebrews 11:3, 8-16*

*Do you have powerful connections?*
4 Little children, you are from God and have overcome them, for he who is in you is greater than he who *is in the world.*
*1 John 4:4-5*

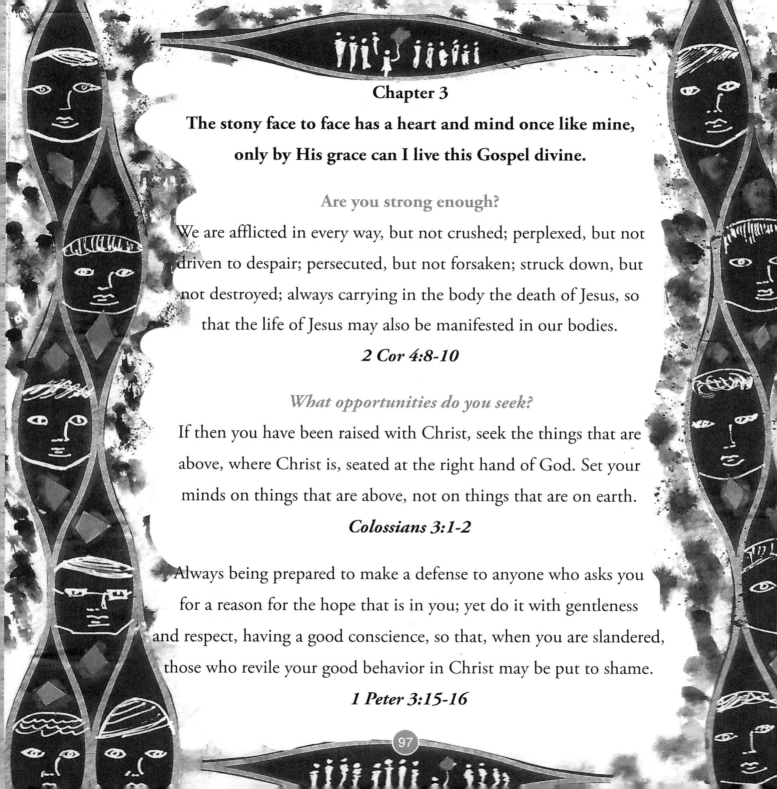

## Chapter 3

**The stony face to face has a heart and mind once like mine,
only by His grace can I live this Gospel divine.**

### Are you strong enough?

We are afflicted in every way, but not crushed; perplexed, but not
driven to despair; persecuted, but not forsaken; struck down, but
not destroyed; always carrying in the body the death of Jesus, so
that the life of Jesus may also be manifested in our bodies.

*2 Cor 4:8-10*

### What opportunities do you seek?

If then you have been raised with Christ, seek the things that are
above, where Christ is, seated at the right hand of God. Set your
minds on things that are above, not on things that are on earth.

*Colossians 3:1-2*

Always being prepared to make a defense to anyone who asks you
for a reason for the hope that is in you; yet do it with gentleness
and respect, having a good conscience, so that, when you are slandered,
those who revile your good behavior in Christ may be put to shame.

*1 Peter 3:15-16*

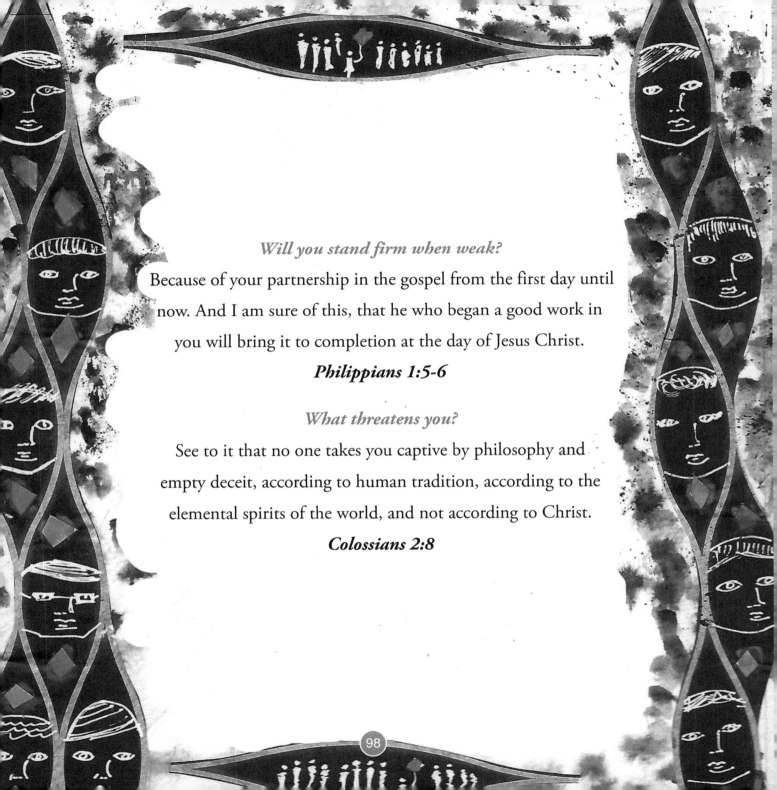

### *Will you stand firm when weak?*

Because of your partnership in the gospel from the first day until now. And I am sure of this, that he who began a good work in you will bring it to completion at the day of Jesus Christ.

**Philippians 1:5-6**

### *What threatens you?*

See to it that no one takes you captive by philosophy and empty deceit, according to human tradition, according to the elemental spirits of the world, and not according to Christ.

**Colossians 2:8**

For the time is coming when people will not endure sound teaching, but having itching ears they will accumulate for themselves teachers to suit their own passions, and will turn away from listening to the truth and wander off into myths.

*2 Timothy 4:3-5*

*Won't you adopt the American culture?*

"No one can serve two masters, for either he will hate the one and love the other, or he will be devoted to the one and despise the other. You cannot serve God and money.

*Matthew 6:24*

Beloved, I urge you as sojourners and exiles to abstain from the passions of the flesh, which wage war against your soul.

*1 Peter 2:11*

**Chapter 4**

**The world hollers lies and lures as I go, but God, your faithfulness and favor is all I want to know.**

*What are your wants?*

And my God will supply every need of yours according to his riches in glory in Christ Jesus.

***Philippians 4:19***

*What need is above all needs?*

But seek first the kingdom of God and his righteousness, and all these things will be added to you.

***Matthew 6:33***

## Friends That Cheered-Me-On...

A whole new generation of Christians has come to believing that it is possible to 'accept' Christ without forsaking the world.

**-Aiden Wilson Tozer**

There is nothing more tragic than to come to the end of life and know we have been on the wrong course.

**-Watchmen Nee**

God always gives His best to those who leave the choice to Him.

**- Jim Elliot**

## Chapter 5

**The Spirit of Truth has built a throne in my heart.**
**He is my refuge and joy, His presence never to depart.**

*Are you weary?*

Come to me, all who labor and are heavy laden, and I will give you rest. Take my yoke upon you, and learn from me, for I am gentle and lowly in heart, and you will find rest for your souls. For my yoke is easy, and my burden is light."

**Matthew 11:28-30**

*Are you thirsty and hungry?*

Jesus said to them, "I am the bread of life; whoever comes to me shall not hunger, and whoever believes in me shall never thirst.

**John 6:35**

Whoever believes in me, as the Scripture has said, 'Out of his heart will flow rivers of living water.'

**John 7:38**

*Why do you miss home?*

"If you love me, you will keep my commandments. And I will ask the Father, and he will give you another Helper, to be with you forever, even the Spirit of truth, whom the world cannot receive, because it neither sees him nor knows him. You know him, for he dwells with you and will be in you.

**John 14:15-17**

For I am sure that neither death nor life, nor angels nor rulers, nor things present nor things to come, nor powers, nor height nor depth, nor anything else in all creation, will be able to separate us from the love of God in Christ Jesus our Lord.

**Romans 8:38-39**

*How is your energy being renewed?*

Abide in me, and I in you. As the branch cannot bear fruit by itself, unless it abides in the vine, neither can you, unless you abide in me. I am the vine; you are the branches. Whoever abides in me and I in him, he it is that bears much fruit, for apart from me you can do nothing.

**John 15:4-9**

# Chapter 6

**Broad is the way to hell, and narrow is heaven's gate.**

**But my steps are ordained by the Lord, I will walk by faith**

*What is the true cost temporary pleasures?*

For what does it profit a man to gain the whole world and forfeit his soul?

*Mark 8:36*

Or do you not know that the unrighteous will not inherit the kingdom of God? Do not be deceived: neither the sexually immoral, nor idolaters, nor adulterers, nor men who practice homosexuality, nor thieves, nor the greedy, nor drunkards, nor revilers, nor swindlers will inherit the kingdom of God.

*1 Cor 6:9-10*

*Are your friends good or godly?*

Blessed is the man[a]

who walks not in the counsel of the wicked,

nor stands in the way of sinners,

nor sits in the seat of scoffers;

but his delight is in the law[b] of the Lord,

and on his law he meditates day and night.

*Psalm 1:1-2*

Do not be deceived: "Bad company ruins good morals.

Is this all there is to life?

**1 Corinthians 15:33**

*Is this all there is to life?*

For this light momentary affliction is preparing for us an eternal weight of glory beyond all comparison, 18 as we look not to the things that are seen but to the things that are unseen. For the things that are seen are transient, but the things that are unseen are eternal.

**2 Corinthians 4:17-18**

*Do you want to be reformed or transformed?*

Therefore, if anyone is in Christ, he is a new creation. The old has passed away; behold, the new has come.

**2 Corinthians 5:17**

3 Do not let your adorning be external—the braiding of hair and the putting on of gold jewelry, or the clothing you wear—4 but let your adorning be the hidden person of the heart with the imperishable beauty of a gentle and quiet spirit, which in God's sight is very precious.

**1 Peter 3:3-4**

*Has God stopped speaking or is your heart too noisy?*

So also no one comprehends the thoughts of God except the Spirit of God. Now we have received not the spirit of the world, but the Spirit who is from God, that we might understand the things freely given us by God. And we impart this in words not taught by human wisdom but taught by the Spirit, interpreting spiritual truths to those who are spiritual. The natural person does not accept the things of the Spirit of God, for they are folly to him, and he is not able to understand them because they are spiritually discerned.

**1 Corinthians 2:11-14**

*How does the world suppress the truth of God?*

For the mind that is set on the flesh is hostile to God, for
it does not submit to God's law; indeed, it cannot.

**Romans 8:7**

Do you not know that friendship with the world is enmity with God? Therefore,
whoever wishes to be a friend of the world makes himself an enemy of God.

**James 4:4**

# Chapter 7

**Biometrics, evidences and answers they seek,**
**all my resources are yours, even the boldness to speak.**

## *Where is your citizenship?*

But our citizenship is in heaven, and from it we await a Savior, the Lord Jesus Christ, who will transform our lowly body to be like his glorious body, by the power that enables him even to subject all things to himself.

*Phil 3:20-21*

So then you are no longer strangers and aliens, but you are fellow citizens with the saints and members of the household of God, built on the foundation of the apostles and prophets, Christ Jesus himself being the cornerstone.

*Ephesians 2:19-20*

## *Why did you come here?*

In the same way, let your light shine before others, so that they may see your good works and give glory to your Father who is in heaven.

*Matthew 5:16*

As it is written, "How beautiful are the feet of those who preach the good news!"

**Romans 10:15**

*Is there a timeline before the deadline?*

And Jesus answered them, "See that no one leads you astray. For many will come in my name, saying, 'I am the Christ,' and they will lead many astray. And you will hear of wars and rumors of wars. See that you are not alarmed, for this must take place, but the end is not yet. For nation will rise against nation, and kingdom against kingdom, and there will be famines and earthquakes in various places. All these are but the beginning of the birth pains.

**Matthew 24:4-8**

Therefore, you also must be ready, for the Son of Man is coming at an hour you do not expect.

**Matthew 24:44**

*Is your visa for heaven pre-approved?*

"For God so loved the world, that he gave his only Son, that whoever believes in him should not perish but have eternal life. For God did not send his Son into the world to condemn the world, but in order that the world might be saved through him.

*John 3:16-18*

For I delivered to you as of first importance what I also received: that Christ died for our sins in accordance with the Scriptures, that he was buried, that he was raised on the third day in accordance with the Scriptures, and that he appeared to Cephas, then to the twelve. Then he appeared to more than five hundred brothers at one time, most of whom are still alive, though some have fallen asleep.

**1 Corinthians 15:3-8**

## Chapter 8

**The highways, byways and tunnels of my heart,**
**God plowed a straight path for me to chart.**

*What is repentance?*

For all have sinned and fall short of the glory of God

***Romans 3:23***

For godly grief produces a repentance that leads to salvation

without regret, whereas worldly grief produces death.

***2 Corinthians 7:10***

Assuming that you have heard about him and were taught in him, as

the truth is in Jesus, to put off your old self, which belongs to your

former manner of life and is corrupt through deceitful desires, and to

be renewed in the spirit of your minds, and to put on the new self,

created after the likeness of God in true righteousness and holiness.

***Ephesians 4:21-24***

*Are you lonely when you are alone?*

"Fear not, for I have redeemed you;

I have called you by name, you are mine.

When you pass through the waters, I will be with you;

and through the rivers, they shall not overwhelm you;

when you walk through fire you shall not be burned,

and the flame shall not consume you.

For I am the LORD your God,

the Holy One of Israel, your Savior.

***Isaiah 43:1-3***

*Are you prepared for sudden loss or trials?*

"Everyone then who hears these words of mine and does them will

be like a wise man who built his house on the rock. And the rain fell,

and the floods came, and the winds blew and beat on that house,

but it did not fall, because it had been founded on the rock.

**Matthew 7:24-25**

*What is the real sense of urgency?*

And just as it is appointed for man to die once, and after that comes judgment

**Hebrews 9:27**

"Seek the Lord while he may be found;

call upon him while he is near;

let the wicked forsake his way,

and the unrighteous man his thoughts;

let him return to the Lord, that he may have compassion on him,

and to our God, for he will abundantly pardon.

For my thoughts are not your thoughts,

neither are your ways my ways, declares the Lord.

For as the heavens are higher than the earth,

so are my ways higher than your ways

and my thoughts than your thoughts.

**Isaiah 55: 6-9**

*What awaits me in future eternity?*

For we must all appear before the judgment seat of Christ, so that each one may

receive what is due for what he has done in the body, whether good or evil.

**2 Corinthians 5:10**

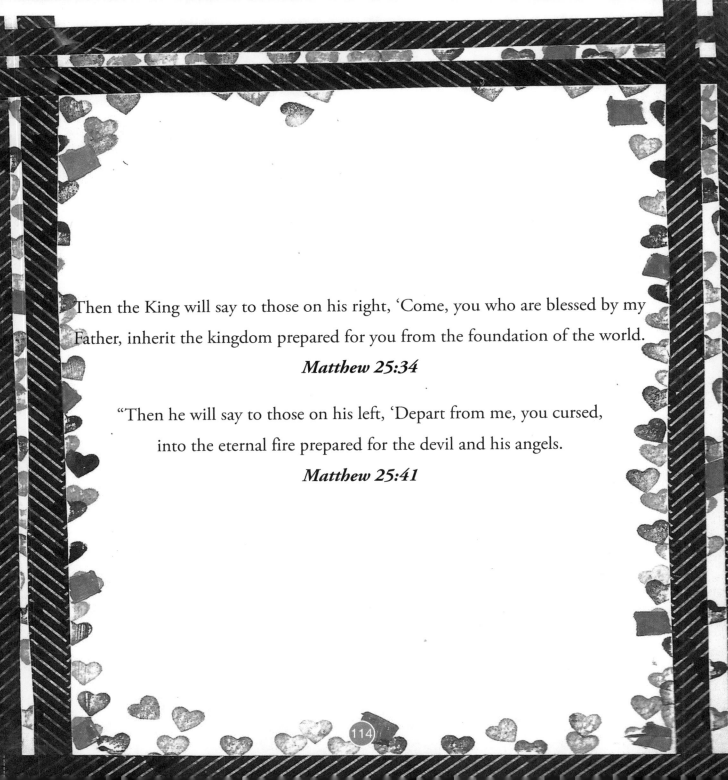

Then the King will say to those on his right, 'Come, you who are blessed by my Father, inherit the kingdom prepared for you from the foundation of the world.

*Matthew 25:34*

"Then he will say to those on his left, 'Depart from me, you cursed, into the eternal fire prepared for the devil and his angels.

*Matthew 25:41*

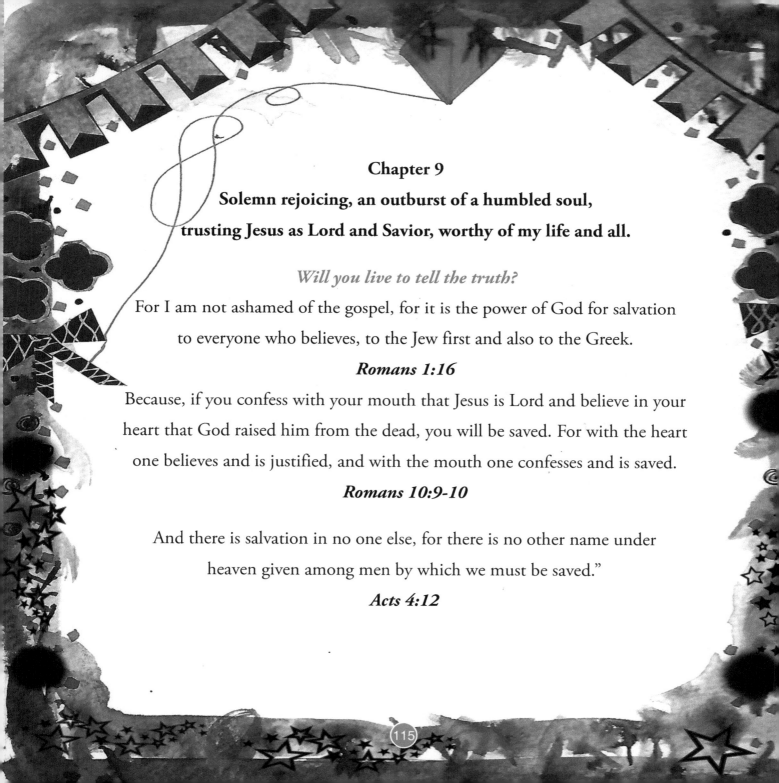

## Chapter 9

### Solemn rejoicing, an outburst of a humbled soul, trusting Jesus as Lord and Savior, worthy of my life and all.

*Will you live to tell the truth?*

For I am not ashamed of the gospel, for it is the power of God for salvation to everyone who believes, to the Jew first and also to the Greek.

*Romans 1:16*

Because, if you confess with your mouth that Jesus is Lord and believe in your heart that God raised him from the dead, you will be saved. For with the heart one believes and is justified, and with the mouth one confesses and is saved.

*Romans 10:9-10*

And there is salvation in no one else, for there is no other name under heaven given among men by which we must be saved."

*Acts 4:12*

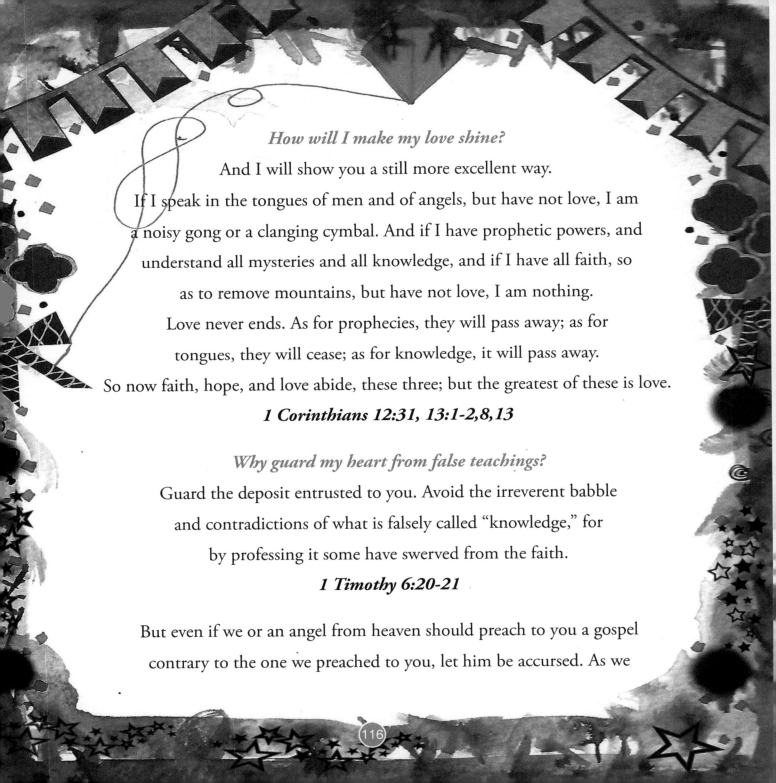

*How will I make my love shine?*

And I will show you a still more excellent way.

If I speak in the tongues of men and of angels, but have not love, I am
a noisy gong or a clanging cymbal. And if I have prophetic powers, and
understand all mysteries and all knowledge, and if I have all faith, so
as to remove mountains, but have not love, I am nothing.

Love never ends. As for prophecies, they will pass away; as for
tongues, they will cease; as for knowledge, it will pass away.

So now faith, hope, and love abide, these three; but the greatest of these is love.

**1 Corinthians 12:31, 13:1-2,8,13**

*Why guard my heart from false teachings?*

Guard the deposit entrusted to you. Avoid the irreverent babble
and contradictions of what is falsely called "knowledge," for
by professing it some have swerved from the faith.

**1 Timothy 6:20-21**

But even if we or an angel from heaven should preach to you a gospel
contrary to the one we preached to you, let him be accursed. As we

have said before, so now I say again: If anyone is preaching to you a gospel contrary to the one you received, let him be accursed.

*Gal 1:8-9*

*Are you eager for Jesus to return?*

In a moment, in the twinkling of an eye, at the last trumpet. For the trumpet will sound, and the dead will be raised imperishable, and we shall be changed.

*1 Corinthians 15:52*

He will wipe away every tear from their eyes, and death shall be no more, neither shall there be mourning, nor crying, nor pain anymore, for the former things have passed away."

*Revelation 21:4*

No longer will there be anything accursed, but the throne of God and of the Lamb will be in it, and his servants will worship him. They will see his face, and his name will be on their foreheads. And night will be no more. They will need no light of lamp or sun, for the Lord God will be their light, and they will reign forever and ever.

*Revelation 22:3-5*

# Chapter 10

**When you melt my heart of stone, my spirit bloomed anew!**

**With a fervent desire to be Christlike, bring honor to You.**

*Do you know Him who truly loves you?*

"For God so loved the world, that he gave his only Son, that whoever believes in him should not perish but have eternal life.

*John 3:16*

*How He came to set you free?*

Have this mind among yourselves, which is yours in Christ Jesus, who, though he was in the form of God, did not count equality with God a thing to be grasped, but emptied himself, by taking the form of a servant, being born in the likeness of men. And being found in human form, he humbled himself by becoming obedient to the point of death, even death on a cross.

*Philippians 2:5-8*

*Of the Holy Spirit's leading…*

6 And because you are sons, God has sent the Spirit of his Son into our hearts, crying, "Abba! Father!" 7 So you are no longer a slave, but a son, and if a son, then an heir through God.

*Galatians 4:6-7*

*to bring us back to God's family.*

He saved us, not because of works done by us in righteousness, but according to his own mercy, by the washing of regeneration and renewal of the Holy Spirit, whom he poured out on us richly through Jesus Christ our Savior, so that being justified by his grace we might become heirs according to the hope of eternal life.

**Titus 3:5-7**

*Will you let the Savior set you free?*

And you, who were dead in your trespasses and the uncircumcision of your flesh, God made alive together with him, having forgiven us all our trespasses, by canceling the record of debt that stood against us with its legal demands. This he set aside, nailing it to the cross. He disarmed the rulers and authorities and put them to open shame, by triumphing over them in him.

**Colossians 2:13-15**

# My Study References

The Holy Bible, King James Version 2010. Grand Rapids, Michigan. Zondervan

MacArthur J. 2010. The MacArthur ESV Study Bible. Wheaton, Illinois, Crossway

MacArthur J. 2009. Fundamentals of the Faith. Chicago, Illinois, Moody Publishers

McGhee V. Thru the Bible with J. Vernon McGee. WWW.ttb.org

# Attribution Page Summary

## Chapter 1

- Image 1–5 (page 2, page 4, page 6, page 8, page 10)
  Collage works and arts, sketches are rendered by A. Guevara, enhanced using Picsart and Paint 3D

## Chapter 2

- Image 6 (page 12)
  World Trade Center, by Khalid Mahmood, Creative Commons
  License:
  Khalid Mahmood (https://commons.wikimedia.org/wiki/File:One_WTC_7.5.13.JPG), "One WTC 7.5.13", Changed filter, color Picsart by A.Guevara, https://creativecommons.org/licenses/by-sa/3.0/legalcode

  Chrysler Building David Shankbone, Creative Commons
  License:
  (https://commons.wikimedia.org/wiki/File:Chrysler_Building_by_David_Shankbone_Retouched.jpg), "Chrysler Building by David Shankbone Retouched", Filter and Color Changes Using Pixart and Paint 3D by A.Guevara, https://creativecommons.org/licenses/by-sa/3.0/legalcode

- Image 7 (page 14)
  Macy's Building—Mike Strand, Creative Commons

- Image 8 (page 16)

- Image 9 (page 18)

(4673314906)", applied filter, cropped using Pixart and or Paint 3D by A.Guevara, https://creativecommons.org/licenses/by/2.0/legalcode

## Chapter 3

- Image 10 (page 20)
  New York City Midtown by Joiseyshowaa, Creative Commons
  License:
  joiseyshowaa @ Flickr (https://commons.wikimedia.org/wiki/File:New_York_City_Empire_State_2010.jpg), "New York City Empire State 2010", filter applied and cropped using Pixart and or Paint 3D by A.Guevara, https://creativecommons.org/licenses/by-sa/2.0/legalcode

- Image 11 (page 22)
  Glory of Commerce Statue, Carol M. Highsmith, Creative Commons
  License:
  Carol M. Highsmith creator QS:P170,Q5044454 (https://commons.wikimedia.org/wiki/File:Architectural_details,_Grand_Central_Station,_New_York,_New_York_LCCN2010630459.tif), "Architectural details, Grand Central Station, New York, New York LCCN2010630459", applied filter, cropped using Pixart and or Paint 3D by A.Guevara, https://creativecommons.org/publicdomain/zero/1.0/legalcode

  Grand Central Station New York, Photo by Fabien Bazanegue on Unsplash

- Image 12 (page 24)
  Flat Iron Building—Author's Own Work, A.Guevara

  The Ring of Mount Apo, Bro. Jeffrey Pioquinto, Creative Commons
  License:
  Bro. Jeffrey Pioquinto, SJ (https://commons.wikimedia.org/wiki/File:The_Ring_of_Mt._Apo.jpg), "The Ring of Mt. Apo", Applied filter, cropped using PixArt and Paint 3D by A.Guevara, https://creativecommons.org/licenses/by/2.0/legalcode

- Image 13 (page 26)
  Federal Hall on Wall Street in New York City, by Hu Totya, Creative Commons
  License:

Hu Totya (https://commons.wikimedia.org/wiki/File:Federal_Hall_front.jpg), "Federal Hall front", Applied filter and cropped using Picsart and or Paint 3D by A.Guevara, https://creativecommons.org/licenses/by-sa/3.0/legalcode

- Image 14 (page 28)
  44th US President, Barrack Obama, Public Domain, Creative Commons
  License:
  Official White House Photo by Pete Souza (https://commons.wikimedia.org/wiki/File:President_Barack_Obama.jpg), "President Barack Obama", Applied filter, changed color and cropped using PixArt by A.Guevara, https://creativecommons.org/publicdomain/zero/1.0/legalcode

  45th US President, Donald Trump, Public Domain, Creative Commons
  License:
  Pacific Southwest Region 5 (https://commons.wikimedia.org/wiki/File:Donald_J._Trump,_45th_President_of_the_United_States_(37521073921).jpg), "Donald J. Trump, 45th President of the United States (37521073921)", Applied filter, changed color and cropped using PicsArt by A.Guevara, https://creativecommons.org/licenses/by/2.0/legalcode

## Chapter 4

- Image 15 (page 30)
  New York City AT Night—Paulo Barcellos Jr, Creative Commons
  License:
  Paulo Barcellos Jr. (https://commons.wikimedia.org/wiki/File:New_York_City_at_night_HDR.jpg), "New York City at night HDR", Filter applied, image cropped using Picsart and Paint3D by A.Guevara, https://creativecommons.org/licenses/by-sa/2.0/legalcode

- Image 16 (page 32)
  New York City AT Night—Paulo Barcellos Jr, Creative Commons
  License:
  Paulo Barcellos Jr. (https://commons.wikimedia.org/wiki/File:New_York_City_at_night_HDR.jpg), "New York City at night HDR", Filter applied, image cropped using Picsart and Paint3D by A.Guevara, https://creativecommons.org/licenses/by-sa/2.0/legalcode

Lamps all over the City by Gnangarra, Creative Commons
License:
Photographs by Gnangarra…commons.wikimedia.org (https://commons.wikimedia.org/wiki/
File:Tranby_house_49_gnangarra.jpg), "Tranby house 49 gnangarra", Enhanced color and cropped
using Picsart and or Paint 3D by A.Guevara, https://creativecommons.org/licenses/by/2.5/au/
deed.en

## Chapter 5

- Image 17 (page 34)
  New York City AT Night—Paulo Barcellos Jr, Creative Commons
  License:
  Paulo Barcellos Jr. (https://commons.wikimedia.org/wiki/File:New_York_City_at_night_HDR.
  jpg), "New York City at night HDR", Filter applied, image cropped using Picsart and Paint3D by
  A.Guevara, https://creativecommons.org/licenses/by-sa/2.0/legalcode

  Autumn trees in Hempstead NY, collage red well, a modified sketch of buildings original works
  by A.Guevara

- Image 18 (page 36)
  Manhattan from Weehawken NJ, by Dmitry Avdeev, Creative Commons
  License:
  Dmitry Avdeev (https://commons.wikimedia.org/wiki/File:Manhattan_from_Weehawken,_
  NJ.jpg), "Manhattan from Weehawken, NJ", Color enhanced and cropped using Picsart and or
  Paint 3D by A Guevara, https://creativecommons.org/licenses/by-sa/3.0/legalcode

  All other images are authors collage works:
  Silver bag owned by author, two picture frames—1) Nephews—Janau, Sydd, Johan and neice Zoe,
  2nd frame—Picture of her and husband when she arrived in the US, April 2016. Furnitures are
  cut-outs and color enhanced from various magazine sources.

- Image in 19 (page 38)
  Collage is original works of Author

Leather Crossway KJV Bible belonging to Author, a picture of the author in her high school days, cut-outs of flowers, fruits and palm trees from various magazine sources, and washi tapes for frames, furniture pieces cut-out from various sources

- Image 20 (page 40)
  Lavenders in Bloom, Oregon, by, icetsarina, Creative Commons
  License:
  (https://commons.wikimedia.org/wiki/File:Lavender_flowers_in_bloom,_Oregon_(35764444215).jpg), "Lavender flowers in bloom, Oregon (35764444215)", filter applied and cropped using Picsart and or Paint 3D by A.Guevara, https://creativecommons.org/publicdomain/zero/1.0/legalcode

All other images are Author's sketch works—The helmet, shield and sword. modified and enhanced using Picsart and or Paint 3D. The bed frame is made from a recycled envelope.

# Chapter 6

- Image 21 (page 42)
  Collage works and arts, sketches are rendered by A.Guevara, enhanced using Picsart and Paint 3D

- Image 22 (page 44)
  Terabass, Times Square New York, Creative Commons
  License:
  Terabass (https://commons.wikimedia.org/wiki/File:New_york_times_square-terabass.jpg), "New york times square-terabass", filter applied, cropped and color enhancements using Picsart and or Paint 3D by A.Guevara, https://creativecommons.org/licenses/by-sa/3.0/legalcode

  All other images are original artwork of A.Guevara
  modified and enhanced sketches using Picsart and or Paint 3D

- Used in Image 23 (page 46)
  Mid-town and Sidewalk in Manhattan—Images owned by A.Guevara
  Collage works and arts, sketches are rendered by A.Guevara, enhanced using Picsart and Paint 3D

- Image 24 (page 48)
  Miznon Restaurant NYC, by Toosu, Creative Commons

License:
(https://commons.wikimedia.org/wiki/File:Miznon_restaurant_NYC_vc.jpg), "Miznon restaurant NYC vc", Filter applied, cropped and color enhanced using Picsart and Paint 3D by A.Guevara, https://creativecommons.org/licenses/by/2.0/legalcode

Collage—Own artwork of A.Guevara and modified sketches and clipped images using Picsart and Paint 3D.

- Image 25 (page 50)
  Radio City, UpstateNYer, Creative Commons
  License:
  UpstateNYer (https://commons.wikimedia.org/wiki/File:Radio_City_Music_Hall_Panorama_BW.jpg), "Radio City Music Hall Panorama BW", Filter applied, color enhanced, cropped using Picsart and or Paint 3D by A.Guevara, https://creativecommons.org/licenses/by-sa/3.0/legalcode

  Collage works and arts, sketches are rendered by A.Guevara, enhanced using Picsart and Paint 3D

- Used in Image 26 (page 52)
  Carnegie Hall, New York, by TROMDOC, Creative Commons
  License:
  TROMDOC (https://commons.wikimedia.org/wiki/File:Carnegie_Hall,_New_York_City,_NY.jpg), Filter applied, color enhanced, cropped using Picsart and or Paint 3 D by A.Guevara, https://creativecommons.org/licenses/by-sa/4.0/legalcode

  Collage works and arts, sketches are rendered by A.Guevara, enhanced using Picsart and Paint 3D

# Chapter 7

- Image 27 (page 54)
  One World Observatory, Night View—by Ronnel Pineda, Hicksville New York

  Collage works and arts, sketches are rendered by A.Guevara, enhanced using Picsart and Paint 3D

- Used in Image 28 (page 56)
  One World Observatory, Day View—by Ronnel Pineda, Hicksville New York

Collage works and arts, sketches are rendered by A.Guevara, enhanced using Picsart and Paint 3D

- Image 29 (page 58)
  Brooklyn Bridge—by Ronnel Pineda, Hicksville New York

  Collage works and arts, sketches are rendered by A.Guevara, enhanced using Picsart and Paint 3D

- Image 30 (page 60)
  Collage works and arts, sketches are rendered by A.Guevara, enhanced using Picsart and Paint 3D

## Chapter 8

- Image 31 (page 62)
  Manhattan, Tero Koistinen, Creative Commons
  License:
  (https://commons.wikimedia.org/wiki/File:Amc_Empire_25_Manhattan_TK.jpg), Filter applied, color enhanced, cropped using Picsart and or Paint 3D by A. Guevara, https://creativecommons. org/licenses/by-sa/4.0/legalcode

  Collage works and arts, sketches are rendered by A.Guevara, enhanced using Picsart and Paint 3D

- Image 32 (page 64)
  Central Park, green trees near body of Water—by Hector Argüello Canals on Unsplash

  Collage works and arts, sketches are rendered by A.Guevara, enhanced using Picsart and Paint 3D

- Image 33(page 66)
  One World Observatory—Ron Pineda, Hickeville New York

  Collage works and arts, sketches are rendered by A.Guevara, enhanced using Picsart and Paint 3D

- Image 34 (page 68)
  New York Botanical Gardens, by King of Hearts, Creative Commons
  License:
  King of Hearts (https://commons.wikimedia.org/wiki/File:New York Botanical Garden October 2016 003.jpg), Filter applied, cropped, color enhanced using Picsart and or Paint 3D by A.Guevara, https://creativecommons.org/licenses/by-sa/4.0/legalcode

Empire State Building, Jiuguang Wang, Creative Commons
License:
(https://commons.wikimedia.org/wiki/File:Empire_State_Building_from_the_Top_of_the_Rock.jpg), "Empire State Building from the Top of the Rock", Filter applied, color enhanced, cropped using Picsart and or Paint 3D by A.Guevara, https://creativecommons.org/licenses/by-sa/2.0/legalcode

Grand Central Station, Photo by Brandon Nickerson on Unsplash

Collage works and arts, sketches are rendered by A.Guevara, enhanced using Picsart and Paint 3D

- Image 35 (page 70)
  Twin Towers, by Lunar Hunter, Creative Commons
  License:
  LunarHunter (https://commons.wikimedia.org/wiki/File:TwinTowersWTC.jpg), Filter Applied, cropped, color enhanced using Picsart and or Paint 3D by A.Guevara, https://creativecommons.org/licenses/by-sa/4.0/legalcode

# Chapter 9

- Image 36 (page 72)
  New York Skyscarper, Image by Pexels from Pixaby
  https://pixabay.com/photos/city-buildings-new-york-skyscrapers-1283300/

Collage works and arts, sketches are rendered by A.Guevara, enhanced using Picsart and Paint 3D

- Image 37 (page 74)
  New York from Empire State View, Black and White by Dietmar Rabich, Creative Commons
  License:
  Dietmar Rabich (https://commons.wikimedia.org/wiki/File:New_York_City_(New_York,_USA),_Empire_State_Building_--_2012_--_6448_(bw).jpg), Filter applied, cropped and enhanced by Picsart and or Paint 3D by A.Guevara, https://creativecommons.org/licenses/by-sa/4.0/legalcode

Collage works and arts, sketches are rendered by A.Guevara, enhanced using Picsart and Paint 3D

- Image 38 (page 78)
  Bethesda Fountation, Central Park New York—by Ronnel Pineda, Hicksville New York

  Collage works and arts, sketches are rendered by A.Guevara, enhanced using Picsart and Paint 3D

- Image 39 (page 76)
  St Patrick's Cathedral, Doreen Saliba, Creative Commons
  License:
  Doreen Saliba 1979 (https://commons.wikimedia.org/wiki/File:St_Patrick's_Cathedral_-_New_York_City.jpg), Filter applied, color enhanced, cropped using Picsart and Paint 3D by A.Guevara, https://creativecommons.org/licenses/by-sa/4.0/legalcode

- Image 40 (page 80)
  New York Brown Building, by Christopher Michel, Creative Commons
  Christopher Michel creator QS:P170,Q5112871 (https://commons.wikimedia.org/wiki/File:In_new_york,_even_the_mundane_is_beautiful_(6773012377).jpg), "In new york, even the mundane is beautiful (6773012377)", Filter applied, color enhanced, cropped using Picsart and or Paint 3D by A. Guevara, https://creativecommons.org/licenses/by/2.0/legalcode

# Chapter 10

- Image 41 (page 82)
  Original: Frédéric Auguste Bartholdi creator QS:P170,Q223274), Public Domain, Creative Commons
  License:
  (https://commons.wikimedia.org/wiki/File:U.S._Patent_D11023.jpeg), "U.S. Patent D11023", Cropped and color enhanced using Picsart and or Paint 3D by A. Guevara, https://creativecommons.org/publicdomain/zero/1.0/legalcode

  Collage works and arts, sketches are rendered by A.Guevara, enhanced using Picsart and Paint 3D

- Image 42 (page 84)
  Bryant Park, New York, Photograph by A.Guevara

  Collage works and arts, sketches are rendered by A.Guevara, enhanced using Picsart and Paint 3D

- Image 43 (page 86)
Manhattan Skyline, Image by Noelsch from Pixabay
Link:
Image by <a href="https://pixabay.com/users/noelsch-136390/?utm_source=link-attribution&utm_medium=referral&utm_campaign=image&utm_content=4582510">noelsch</a> from <a href="https://pixabay.com/?utm_source=link-attribution&utm_medium=referral&utm_campaign=image&utm_content=4582510">Pixabay</a>

Collage works and arts, sketches are rendered by A.Guevara, enhanced using Picsart and Paint 3D

# About the Author

*A*nna Jean Pardillo-Guevara was born in Cebu, Philippines. In 2013, she became a Christian, and developed a growing desire to study God's Word. She served cheerfully in ministries at World in Need Baptist Church.

She moved to New York in 2016, nurturing the same love for the Bible and willingness to serve. The same love blossomed into a creativity encouraged by her husband, Robert.

She now serves as a Sunday School Teacher for Crossbridge Baptist Church, Westbury, New York.

She would love to hear from you. Email her at A.Guevara_MMXX@outlook.com

CPSIA information can be obtained
at www.ICGtesting.com
Printed in the USA
BVHW021623300820
587632BV00004B/38